Northborough C.P. School,
Church Street,
Northborough,
Peterborough.

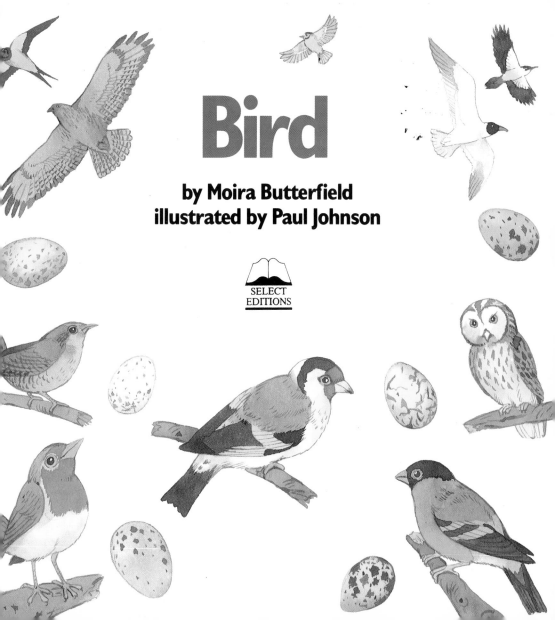

# Bird

## by Moira Butterfield
## illustrated by Paul Johnson

SELECT
EDITIONS

A little bird builds a nest.

There are many different kinds of nests. This one is shaped like a cup.

It is made from roots
and moss. The inside
is covered with soft
down.

When the nest is finished, the little bird lays some eggs.

The nest will help to keep them safe.

The little bird sits on the eggs to keep them warm.

Her mate brings her food, so she doesn't have to leave the nest.

Around each egg
there is a hard shell.
It has tiny holes all
over it to let air
through.

Inside each egg there is a yolk. In the yolk there is a tiny spot that will grow into a chick.

Around the yolk
there is some white.
It has a store of
water for the chick.

The chick begins to grow inside the egg. It gets food from the yolk.

Soon the chick begins to look like a bird.

Slowly it grows wings, feet, and a beak.

When the chick is ready, it chips a hole in the eggshell.

It makes the hole
bigger and bigger.
At last the shell
breaks open.

These chicks are small and helpless. They must stay in the nest.

Their parents bring them food.

Soon they begin to grow feathers.

When they are big enough, they will fly away. One day they may build nests of their own.